Straightening Her Crown

Compiled by Cheryl Barton

Contributing Writers

Cheryl Barton
Nichole M. Wallace
Sally Quon
Shannon Scott
Terry Beamon
Tamara N. Harvey
JoAnn Wilson
Jill Ocone
Treesa "Poesis" Boyce-Gaither
Michele Mekel

About

Welcome to *"Straightening Her Crown"*, a testament that not all women see each other as competition, but as a means to a smile. This book anthology is a symbol of love and devotion to seeing all women soar. Helping a woman keep her crown straight is not about self, but about being selfless with your heart. What is her crown? It's not just a jeweled tiara on her head. It's her self-esteem, her wealth, her health, her well-being; it's her *life*. It's everything that a woman is that, at times, may not represent her at her best.

In this anthology, we are women who are excited to share a few encouraging words to help another woman get back on track, to put a smile on her face, to allow her to see that she is not alone in her struggles – that we're all here for her. Take a journey with these ten women who make up this anthology, and if even one word blesses your life, we have done what we set out to do; support and encourage. It is our hope that you will share these words with family and friends and if you can, with a sister-friend who could use some inspiration.

Dedication

I dedicate this anthology to every woman who, without any hesitation, would help another woman keep her crown on straight. Thank you for being exactly what another woman, another sister needs.

This book is also provided in dedication to my cousin, *Andrea Denise Gentry*. I miss you dearly. You listened to my secrets and my dreams and kept them close. When I would go left, you pulled me to the right, helping to keep me centered. You were my crown straightener. When I feel it slipping these days, I imagine you fixing it just right and telling me to keep my head up so that it never slips again. I hold dear, our heart to heart over breakfast one morning during the "Women Thou Art Loosed" Florida conference. We had so many plans that were left unfulfilled. I'm watching my crown and I appreciate the time we had together as cousins but more like sisters. Rest sweetly in heaven, until we meet again.

Cheryl

Acknowledgments

Thank you to the women who thought it not robbery of their time and talents to lend their words to this project. I continue on this path to inspire, empower and encourage because of women like you! Thank you a million times over! I am because of you.

Terry Beamon
Treesa "Poesis" Boyce-Gaither
Tamara N. Harvey
Michele Mekel
Jill Ocone
Sally Quon
Shannon Scott
Nichole M. Wallace
JoAnn Wilson

Table of Contents

The Miseducation of an Intelligent
Black Queen
Treesa "Poesis" Boyce-Gaither

There's Still Water in the Well
Terry Beamon

One Choice
Michele Mekel

Hit the Reset Button
Cheryl Barton

Closing
Shannon Scott

YOU
Treesa "Poesis" Boyce-Gaither

Hey Sis,

You ok? You haven't been looking like yourself lately. I know it feels like the world is on your shoulders but understand, it doesn't go unnoticed. People expect you to be Superwoman...Wonder woman, but I am here to remind you that even Shero's need a break.

Sis, it's ok to say NO... it's ok to say NOT TODAY... it's okay to take the world off your shoulders. Trust me, everyone will be fine. Who takes care of the person that takes care of everyone else? Instead of trying to figure that out, take time for yourself. Eat your favorite food, drink your favorite drink, watch the movie of your choice, and even if you must...cry, scream, let it all out. Just don't forget to BREATHE! It's ok Sis! Show them your smile when you are ready. The world owes you nothing, yet they owe you everything. So, Queen, here, take these flowers today. We are all here standing at your side in solidarity, and at your back holding you up for those days when you feel weak. Take some time for you. We may not speak much but Sis, I appreciate you and I see you.

Love,

Sis.

The Soul of This Woman
Cheryl Barton

My ears can hear you,
but no words are spoken.
My heart can feel you,
yet, there is no touch.
My mind can see you,
yet, you're faceless.
My soul connects with yours,
our hurt is the same.
We fall, then rise the same,
we proclaim our victory together.
Our relevance in this world links us in a
bond that's too deep to be destroyed.
The soul of *this* woman holds me high
and lifts you up so you can soar.

My heart beats, playing a tune that my
ancestors understand.
My life is lived on the dreams they
wished for but didn't live to see.
I smile today knowing a dream deferred
is now meant for me.
My soul longs to break free to embrace

fresh, new souls.

It speaks of a woman who has walked some rough roads.

I love as hard as I live, I hold on as tight as I can.

I tell the stories from my heart where my soul lives, yeah, where it all began.

The soul of *this* woman can't be silenced nor will it be contained.

It spreads far and wide like wings on an eagle, it remembers the struggles of the past.

It fights to merge what is now, with what was then.

I *AM* the soul of *THIS* woman; the fight for my soul to win will never end.

In Search of Joy
Michele Mekel

One day, I looked around, and she was gone.
No forwarding address had been left.

I couldn't file a missing person report.
She had no SSN or state ID.

In fact, no one else would know where to look.
I was her only kith and kin—the only one who
really knew her.

There was none but me to notice her retreat.
But the chasm of her departure was clear to
all—no smiling eyes, no bubbling bliss.

So I sleuthed and sought in favorite haunts, in
all my avocations.
I panned for clues in the river of memories and
the stream of dreams.

On the trail, there've been plenty of dead ends
and false leads.
But there are also glimpses of where she's been
and where she's headed next.

It's Time to Make a Move
Nichole M. Wallace

Women are known for making a move that morphs into a movement. We are motivators, encouragers, delegators and instructors. Since the beginning of time, we have had to be the queens of multi-tasking. We take the lead at home, at work and in our communities. We wear multiple hats, spin plates, juggle balls, and do it effortlessly.

I am reminded of the classic 1970's perfume that made everyone want to be the Enjoli woman. I am showing my age here, but the jingle to the song chanted about being a woman who could *"bring home the bacon, fry it up in a pan, and never let you forget you're a man."* Again, I say women have been making moves and turning them into movements since the beginning of time. Some may have considered us radical for working outside of the home. Others, have called us rebels for taking on positions in the board room and the battlefield that were previously delegated as "For Men Only". As a result, we have been coined as bad mama jamma's, divas, or boss chicks. No matter the title, from the beginning of time women have demonstrated that we can do all things and do them well!

Women stand in the gap and are known for moving in untraditional ways to invoke change in ourselves and those we come in contact with. We are creative. We can make a gourmet meal from the scraps from our cupboard. We are thrifty. We can repurpose hand me downs into an outfit worthy of the front page of *Vogue*. We are way makers and trendsetters most capable of taking nothing and make it into something. Again, I say women have been known to make moves that morph into movements.

Webster's dictionary defines a movement as a series of organized activities working toward an objective. Some moves are deliberate. Some moves are spontaneous. Some moves are intentional. Some moves are forced. Some moves are planned publicly, some are made behind closed doors, and others at kitchen tables. Some moves are made in silence and without pomp and circumstance. Others have voices that can be heard via airways and read over pages.

You're never too old to make a move. At the age of 72, after 60 years of Missionary work and receiving a Nobel Peace Prize, Mother Theresa was able to secure a cease fire during the Siege of Beirut. Her negotiations as a part of "Operation Peace for Galilee" secured the rescue of 37 disabled children who were being held captive.

You're never too young to make a move. In 2019, at the age 14, Marsai Martin became Hollywood's youngest executive producer with the blockbuster hit "Little". Currently worth millions, this destined billionaire has won countless awards from Phenom, BET, and the NAACP.

Pedigree does not prohibit your ability to move. Oprah Winfrey was so poor as a child that she was teased for wearing potato sack dresses. She has gone on to become a well-respected actress, journalist and multimedia mogul. She is known for landing interviews with stars and dignitaries that no one else can. Most recently, she secured the well-publicized interview with Prince Harry and his wife the Duchess of Sussex after stepping down from their royal responsibilities. Oprah currently has a net worth of $2.5 billion and has been a benefactor to many.

Regardless, of age, race, or social stature, women have made moves that changed the trajectory of their lives and the outlook of those around them. You have met these women. They are your mothers, grandmothers, and teachers. You have raised these women. They are your daughters and nieces. Sisters...you are these women. You have changed lives. You have made a difference. Yet, there is still more work that you have been tasked to do. Unfortunately, life and all its dimensions can sometimes take the wind from out of our sails. We can get so bogged down helping others accomplish their goals and dreams that we forget about working toward our own. That is until one day you look up and ask what happened to your dream and how did it become deferred.

What's stopped you from making your move? You know, that step toward that vision, dream, or goal. Was it fear? What is it that is preventing you from reaching that goal you have put on the back burner or actualizing the vision you had of doing something new and fresh? Is it the children who are grown now? Did doubt step in and make you concerned that you would not be successful?

Movement is critical to your success. Where there is movement, there is gain. Even backwards moves referred to as setbacks have their purpose. Setbacks offer the time for you to recharge, regroup, and then reapply new techniques to those which challenged your success.

What move have you been tasked to make yet have been reluctant to get started on? You know that nagging thought or vision that just won't go away. Is it going back to school? Starting a business? Organizing a community project? Maybe, you've been called into ministry. Perhaps your heart is heavy with the task of activism and being a change agent in the community. Are you tasked to learn an instrument, write a book, start a business, serve the homeless, start a training program? Maybe you are supposed to take on the reigns as matriarch of your family, adopt a child, or make a new product. Whatever the thought, the ball has been placed in your court and you will not score the points unless you start moving toward the net and take your best shot. Sister, it is time to make a move. You've sat on the sidelines long enough. You've gotten your second wind. Get back in the game.

Where there is no movement there is stagnation. Where there is stagnation there is atrophy. Where there is atrophy there is loss. Where there is loss, there is death. Make a move sisters so you do not lose your peace, your purpose, or your position. If you don't make a move, you will spend the rest of your days wondering what would have happened if you did. If you don't make a move, a piece of you will get loss in the shadows of what could have been. If you don't make a move, you will find yourself out of the game.

If you are going to make a move it will require action. All you need to do is formulate a plan. What have you been tasked to do? Where are those tasks supposed to occur? Why have you been tasked with doing it? Who are those tasks going to benefit? Is there a current void in that area? Are there others that do what you plan to do? What makes them successful? What are their challenges? When is the best time to implement this venture? In business, the technical term for this is market research. A simpler thought is this, do your homework and know what is needed for you to deliver and deliver effectively.

I know these are a lot of questions but their answers are the foundation for your success. You see, the answers to these questions are the blueprint for your implementation plan. That being the case, I want to remind you of what I said earlier. Some moves are spontaneous. Spontaneous moves are instinctive and when moving on instinct you have to strike while it's hot. Thus, in some instances all those plans we just talked about may not be needed or some of them may get thrown out the window. To that end, don't over think things. Instead, be willing to make a move when the timing is right even if you feel you may not be prepared.

Once you make a move, you must be prepared to fight through the friction. Where there is movement, there is friction. Friction is the resistance that one surface or object encounters when moving over another. When you make a move, someone may oppose it. They may not understand your perspective or the need. They may even consider you as a threat. As a result, they may make it their purpose to keep you from accomplishing your goals. When that occurs, be prepared to dig in deep so that you are not swayed by the opposition. It is important to note that opposition is not all bad. Opposition sharpens you. It helps you refine your methods and can even re-purpose you as you recall why you started on the journey to begin with.

Sisters, friction is what is considered a necessary evil. Friction causes heat and where there is heat there may be damage. I urge you to insulate yourself with people, places, and things that can protect you from friction's damages. Where there is heat, there is purging. Where there is purging, there becomes room for expansion. Expansion means growth. Don't be discouraged by the friction. Instead, develop thick skin so the impact of friction's blows are not as painful. You may not always like the feedback you hear or see. Your objective may ruffle feathers but friction comes with movement. If you were called to action, there is a purpose to be served. Allow that purpose to fuel the flames for the friction. Heat makes an object more susceptible to change. It's in the heat that barriers are broken and entryways are made. Movement and friction are a necessary duo.

It is important to note that a lot of energy is sometimes spent to overcome friction before an object even starts to move. You may encounter naysayers before you ever start. There may be delays and disruptions but don't become disillusioned. Stay focused. Keep your eyes set on the path ahead so you can stay the course and not get tossed off the road you have been destined to travel. Remember why you started and keep moving.

In the movies, every time the protagonist makes a major transition, theme music is traditionally played to signify that a transition is on the way. When the friction becomes the worst, what theme music will you play to help you stay the course? Will you look at the opposition, demand R.E.S.P.E.C.T. and make sure to TCB? Even though you may be afraid and petrified, will you be able to tell yourself "I Will Survive"? Are you "Every Woman"? If so, stay the course because it's all in you. "Believe in Yourself" right from the start, not because I told you to, but because no one can change the path that you must go. The power inside you is greater than the forces around you. That power is guiding you. That power gives you your strength. It is a "Strength like no other" and it reaches to you. In the fullness of His grace and the power of His name, that strength will lift you up. That power will allow you to live your life and be "Just Fine".

Make a move and don't stay still. Make that move sister and get your inheritance. Future generations are depending on you, the system needs to hear your voice, there is a current void that only you can fill. Remember, one move is all it takes. One move will morph into movement. The wait is over. Walk into your season. On your mark, get set, go! Make that move right now!

Women
Shannon Scott

The value of a woman should not be determined by the shape of her body or the way her face looks.

The media has filled our heads with images of beautiful women who look nothing like you or me, so, in our heads, that's what we need to be. We forget value is more important than beauty, so, no matter how much changing you do to yourself, if you don't love yourself, how can anyone else?

A woman is valued by the respect she has for herself.

So, what is a woman?

We are the gatekeepers to emotion.

We are the multiplier of life.

The fighters of love.

We are the cycle breakers, the caretakers.

We are the glue that keeps the family together.

We are the problem solvers.

We are the strength to keep going even when all odds are against us.

We are the peace when there is a full war going on outside.

We are the prize.

Straighten Your Crown Queen
Tamara N. Harvey

Straighten your crown **Queen**!
It is a symbol
Of Power and Dignity.

You deserve the best,
Remind yourself that you do,
Now and forever.

I am here for you!
When you need your crown straightened
Please be there for me.

Nothing can break me,
Not even a pandemic
Can wither my faith.

The Conversation
Treesa "Poesis" Boyce-Gaither

Hello,

I haven't seen you in a minute and you look different to me. Almost certain one of us is a new person but the face I can't see. Dressed in the same clothes but yours seem worn down; I have waved and smiled but you ignored me and frowned. I tried to start a conversation with you, but you shunned away as if I was something to fear. I caught you crying and attempted to wipe away your tears. You told me I have been neglecting you so in your direction I stayed clear. I missed you and I just needed to talk. Need to vent to get somethings off my chest. My life is falling apart, I'm confused things are a mess. You look so sad and dull and not yourself, like a book someone used to read, dusty on a shelf. I can't find you, please make yourself seen, I need a reason to believe...in me.

My Dear Queen,

I am a reflection of you, an image of your soul that's been abused. I have always been here through your smile and tears. I have been here through your strengths and fears. I have answered when you cried out; I have offered you peace, though you blocked me out. I showed you trust, despite your doubt. I watch you on bended knees hiding pieces of you in the soil. I am your muse, and to the victor goes the spoil! I have been here for years, picking apart your thoughts, eliminating your doubts, and preparing your plot. You fear the touch of the quill and the blankness of the canvas; just trust yourself and let the words manifest. I promise it may not make sense now, just start with one word and the pen will make a sound. So much conversation can be had but talk to me, it doesn't matter if you're mad.

I am your muse, the reflection of you, violate my mind and make me...NEW!

Shout, Shout
Cheryl Barton

Shout with a voice of triumph that signals where you're headed and not just from how far you've come.

Shout with a desire to be heard because you have something to say that could change a generation.

Shout in the midst of a great storm and watch the torrential waters cease as they stop to fear your determination to push through in spite of.

Shout to confirm that you can actually hear your own voice and remember, you have one.

Go ahead and shout! Shout it out! Be heard! Be seen!

Shout and then stand tall. That sound released a thousand levels of pent-up frustration.

And now, take that next powerful step because you are on your way to begin again.

On Cougar Annie, Lynda and Me
Sally Quon

A book came for me in the mail yesterday. "Cougar Annie's Garden" by Margaret Horsfield. I looked at the cover for just a minute and then I set it aside. This book is highly special to me. I want to save it for a time that I can savour every word, commit to every sentence. It was recommended to me by someone who made a deep and lasting impression on me, even though I only knew her for a short while.

I met Lynda on the 6th of August. She was dying. Terminal cancer riddled her body and I'd been asked to spend the night with her at her home when she was released from the hospital - just in case she needed something. She had very little time left.

We had a rough start. Lynda was extremely sensitive to scent, and even though I was careful to shower without soap and not apply anti-perspirant, my clothing had a mild scent left behind from the laundry detergent. Lynda's sister did some scrambling to find something of Lynda's I could wear while leaving my own shirt hanging outside in the yard. Once that was taken care of, her sister left for her own home and family. Lynda and I were alone.

"Would you like me to stay with you or would you prefer some quiet time?" I asked.

"There have been so many people in and out. Not a moment's peace. I would love it if I could just close my eyes and be left alone," she said.

I told her to call out if she needed me, and I left the room. The tumors in Lynda's brain made her very sensitive to light as well as scent. The house was dark, even in the early evening. I made my way down the hall to the kitchen. Not two minutes passed before Lynda called me. She asked me to feed her cats and make sure that they had enough water. She kept bowls on the floor throughout the house, so that wherever they were, they would have access to water. I'm a firm believer in the fact that a person's character can be judged by the way they treat animals. Lynda was obviously someone who took great care of the two cats that shared her home. As ill as she was, her first thought was for her pets, rather than herself. When the task was complete, I returned to the kitchen, prepared to spend the night working on a project I'd brought from home.

"Sally!" she called out again and I knew. Lynda didn't want to be alone. She was afraid. She just didn't want to say so. Without comment, or acknowledgement of any kind, I pulled a chair up beside her bed.

The night passed. We sat together in the darkness, talking softly. I put cold towels on her feet to reduce the swelling. I held her upright in an odd embrace, patting her back as if I were burping a baby. It helped her to breathe. She rested her head on my shoulder. We shared stories – very personal stories. My admiration for her grew with every word she spoke. She told me of her life, the jobs she'd had, the men she'd loved. The stories of her grandmother that she'd never shared with anyone before. I shared with her the story of my escape from an abusive marriage, and my fears that I wouldn't be able to live up to the task of starting over.

"I don't want to die," she said, abruptly. "There are things I still want to do."

A moment passed.

"Are you ready to die?" she asked. Up until six months ago, I truly thought I was going to die. All that had changed.

"I feel like I've only just started to live," I answered honestly.

"Yes," she said, "I can see that."

In the darkness her hand sought mine. Somehow, I already knew, and was waiting.

"I wish I didn't have to die," Lynda said. She squeezed my hand weakly. "Thank you for being here. You're so strong."

Me? Strong? That was the last word I'd use to describe myself.

"You remind me of Cougar Annie. Have you ever read that book? It's one of my favourites. I wish I could give it to you, but

I loaned it to someone and never got it back."

"I'd love to read it."

"Promise me you will."

"I promise."

She leaned back on her pillows. She told me about Cougar Annie, how she had come to this country and carved a niche from the unforgiving wilderness. How she had outlived four husbands, raised a family, ran a post office and a mail-order business. How she protected herself and her land from the cougars that roamed the area. Cougar Annie was a force to be reckoned with. She was strong, independent and tough as nails. I thought she sounded a lot like Lynda.

We didn't speak much more after that. Lynda was tired. I held her when she needed to be held, brought a glass to her lips when she needed to drink, and sang softly when the night was the darkest.

In the morning, I left. Lynda was sleeping peacefully, her breath finally calm and even. I stopped at the beach to watch the sun rise and thought about Cougar Annie, Lynda and me.

I didn't know that someone as broken as I was had anything to offer anyone, yet Lynda thought I was strong for having walked away from everything I had ever known. I thought she was the bravest person I'd ever met. I'd never known anyone who could face their own end with such poise and grace.

Somewhere in the darkness of the night, each of us had found something we needed, each of us had given something to the other. It was as though together we formed a well that each of us could draw upon. I was stronger because of her. She was braver because of me. It was powerful, mysterious, and very feminine.

As I watched the sun crest the mountains, I knew that this incredible power the two of us had created was right there, not just for me, but for all women. If we could find a way to set aside petty behaviour, hold hands and put our minds and spirits to the task, we could accomplish anything. *Anything*. It's no wonder that women have historically been charged with witchcraft. It's no wonder that women were once feared by the patriarchy. I may have been tired, and my eyes may have been grainy, but I had never seen anything so clearly in my life.

I felt like a new person, woven from the strands of Lynda's courage, Cougar Annie's legacy of strength and my own resilience. For the first time in more than 25 years, I felt like I was in complete control of my life. I knew I was going to be just fine. Lynda had given me a gift, and I was not going to waste it.

I ordered "Cougar Annie's Garden" as soon as I got home.

Lynda died before I could read it.

I miss her.

Note
Shannon Scott

A woman must first learn her value.
From there, she can form a legacy.
From the creation of her legacy,
she gains power.

"God, I Trust You; It's Me I Don't Trust"
Terry Beamon

Inspired by Mark 9:14-29

When I think about the man in the story in the Bible of Mark 9, that had the son with the evil spirit who was unable to speak at all, and his father asked the disciples to help drive out the evil spirit that his son was consumed with, I think about how, for so long, I had been functioning in such dysfunction since I was a child. I am not sharing this story or any of my writings in this book for a pity party, but I am in a season where God is telling me that I have to be transparent for my healing, as well as other's healing to take place. You see, for so long, I believed that if I go to God in prayer, He would automatically answer my prayers. Not the prayers for myself; I was, at that time, not to ask for anything for myself because I did not want God to think I was selfish in prayer, but to pray the prayers for persons that I knew and did not know. Yes, the saved and the unsaved, the functional and the dysfunctional. I would cry out to God in secret, and at that time, not having a personal relationship with Him but thinking that if I prayed, He would answer. As I got older, no longer crying out like when I was a child, I would see Pop and Grandma praying and they were God fearing grandparents that were in my life. I would see their prayers being answered. But God showed me something as they prayed. Fasting, Pop would give up sweets and grandma, before she got sick, would give up Double Mint Gum and that Apple Tobacco.

Through their prayers and fasting, God showed me that He is not a *SUGAR DADDY* that jumps and answers every prayer request. I learned that I have to reach out to him with knowing that it also takes FAITH, PRAYING, and FASTING for some things to change. There have been times that God has not changed the situations and our problems may not be an evil spirit in us but sometimes, God gives us the strength, as I shared in the beginning of this writing, to be functional in dysfunction. Trust God with your prayers, no matter what His answer may be.

I Dare You To...
Cheryl Barton

Year, 2020, taught us all a lot of lessons about the things we can and cannot control. If you were paying attention, you saw ways to appreciate all that you have and to take nothing for granted. A virus showed up and shut the world down, literally. What some thought would come and go and be as normalized as the common cold or the flu, actually came to town, took a seat, grabbed the remote control and some snacks, scratched itself here and there and decided to become the thing that wouldn't leave. You know, like that family member who shows up at your house uninvited and decides to make themselves at home; again, uninvited. Were you one of the people who told that virus that it wasn't welcome here? I sure was, but that didn't stop it from wreaking havoc on our lives.

Like so many others, I came into 2020 with high hopes for newness; good newness, not the mayhem that ensued. Still, I am good at learning how to cope with life in a stressful environment. I thought that 2020 was going to be the year that I would travel more than I ever had. I wanted to go to concerts in different states, head back to Los Angeles, my favorite spot, maybe a few trips to Florida, a few day and weekend trips to the beach and just really get out in the world more. Being an introvert, that's a lot for me, but I had set myself up for the challenge. After all, I had worked hard to be able to do some of those things. A lot of us did. 2020 was going to be my year. I can almost hear you say the same words as you are reading this.

It started off with me deciding to purchase a new home. Where I should probably downsize a little, I decided to go a little bigger, able to squeeze in my closing at the end of February, literally before everything began to shut down. I thought I had mapped out the perfect plan for my year; move into my new home, do some decorating while also taking all the trips I strategically planned for myself through the end of the year, six in all.

First up was a concert in New York with one of my greatest, bestest friends in the world, Clarissa. I got on the road, headed off to see Jill Scott, one of my favorite musical artists. Kicking off her show was DJ DNice, and we all now know the amazing impact he's had on our lives with this *Club Quarantine* or CQ, music sets. It was a great time in New York and I was so ready for more, much, much more. I came back home, prepared for settlement the next day all the while, the world was changing. Lives were changing and not according to plan like I had for mine. The virus, this COVID-19, had made its way to the United States and we weren't prepared. The country wasn't ready for the many, many lives that would be lost. We weren't ready for businesses and services to completely close and for people to be shut-in like never before in our lives. What was happening?

Well, what happened was the sign of the time was survival. It was no longer planning for a spring and summer of travel, but on a mission, instead, to find face masks, hand sanitizer and wipes. Yes, my mission for my life in 2020 changed significantly. Like during a winter snow storm, shelves in stores were vacant of bottled water, food, paper towels and many other essentials. People lived in terror of a virus not many knew about and that no one could control. Lives were being lost in high numbers. Hospital staff, not know what they were encountering, were not immediately protected and so their lives were being placed in jeopardy each day, many of those essential workers succumbing to the same deadly virus. The world began to pray for help and many began to question why.

I'm not usually a worrier, instead I usually choose to find my way through. I was lost. I held my shoulders high, my chest poked out and my mind raced with what to do. I started to hear that the virus seemed to attack our seniors more than anyone else, as well as those with preexisting medical conditions. We thought the virus was targeting those with health issues and so we became a world of checking our health. We donned masks, some even within our own households. I found myself doing supermarket runs for my parents because the last thing I wanted was for them to be out putting themselves at risk just to find life's essential items.

Have you ever put yourself at risk, having more concern for someone else other than yourself? That was me. My only concern was figuring out what I needed to do to keep my parents safe. What I began to notice was I had to go inside my parents' house, wearing a mask and they had to stay on another level of the house waving at me as if I was a stranger. It wasn't their fault or my fault, but it was how our lives had to be in order for me to keep them safe. I did what I had to do and I hated it. I wasn't use to being a daughter who made a quick stop and then off again. I didn't like having to talk to them from a different level of the house. Yeah, hated that too. The start of 2020 was rough, but still, I dared myself to find the silver lining because I believe, in everything thing, there is one. In 2020, what was that silver lining you say? Let me break it down for you.

That silver lining became, in spite of what

was happening in the world, I was able to still work from home while I prayed without ceasing for those who were not as lucky. I was thankful for that while others struggled with how to survive. I wasn't working from because of the virus. I've been teleworking everyday for quite a few years, so not much about that part of my life had changed.

My silver lining was I was out in these streets, taking care of my parents the way, they took care of me as I was growing into womanhood, and even after that. I took pride in knowing that I could and so I did, without hesitating.

The silver lining was that I had made new on-line friends and connected with those who loved reading romance and inspirational novels at a level that I had not seen since I published my first book in 2013. I was rejuvenated to write more, give more, connect more.

The silver lining was that God kept my sanity in place because I watched the spirits and confidence in so many take a nose-dive.

A lot of people found they didn't do well if they were not out and about interacting with a lot of people. I found myself in a perfect niche as an introvert. I now found that I didn't have to make excuses for not venturing out to be in groups of people when I didn't really want to, though that was being anti-social. I found comfort in the place of peace I found in the midst of the storm. Still, I prayed for extroverts. The stay-at-home orders were a struggle for many of them.

The silver lining was I found time to learn more about myself and appreciate all that I had. I'm not speaking of material things, but more of the preciousness of life. Like many, I've walked through days not appreciating the gift of every twenty-four hours. I assumed another twenty-four hours would show up after the last and it was what it was. It would be another day. In 2020, each day was a true gift, especially when you watched the news or checked social media to see another thousand or so lives lost since the last twenty for hours and that was just in one state. 2020 was a sad time, but that meant that when 2021 hit, oh, how differently did that hit. 2021 sent me into an, "I Dare You To" mindset. I had survived 2020 and I felt dared to survive 2021 with gusto. Me? I accepted that challenge. I see my life differently now.

When I originally set out to do so many things in 2020, I am now daring myself to still do those things. The world is still a scary place, but I feel dared to venture out into it knowing that I need to carry myself through each day saying, thank you. What about you? Are you ready? Are you set? I dare you to walk each day with a new zest from this day forward.

I dare you to go out and smell the roses, even with cicadas all over them. They still smell fresh and clean.

I dare you to go to the supermarket, stand in line and great the person in front of and behind you with a smile and a small wave because you're all looking into faces of survivors.

I dare you to fix what's broken and be ready to heal again. What seemed easy to not forgive and not forget should be looked at different in 2021. What seemed like a mountain in the past should make you feel like you can leap it in a single bound. Go ahead and try!

I dare you to start that new project and push through to that new goal. Chase it down, throw it to the ground and rule it like a boss!

I dare you to pull out that to-do list and go through it with a determination that your life will be lived with each scratch-off.

I dare you to make a plan and even if a virus hits this world again, you know that you have survived before and you will again.

I dare you to dream a bigger dream than you have in the past and do it. Just do it.

I dare you.

The Power
Shannon Scott

It sounds scary when it's said aloud.

It makes you think that power is the force that I have over you.

Actually, it's the power that runs through you that I am speaking of.

It is the courage and will to move like only you know how to in order to solve the biggest problems in the world and still make it home on time.

A power to not let your past define you or hold you in an hourglass of past sins.

A power that is not about money or clout.

A power that cannot be snatched away.

A power that is infused with self-worth and

respect.

A power that knows the difference between love and a future ending of regret.

Real power is embracing who you are and loving every bit of it.

It's embarking on a journey to line up who you are with what you do.

True power is taking the time you are given in life and dominating any dream that you want to.

Real power is to have an appreciation for the contributions that you can bring way before you can hear a hand clap.

Did y'all understand that?

My Crown
JoAnn Wilson

At the beginning of 2017, my crown was on straight, shining, and bright. I had written my first book at the age of 66, which was a dream come true and was supported by family and friends. By the end of that year, my crown was askew, tarnished and on a shelf. You see, I lost my mom, and I wasn't even interested in a crown. I was lost, alone and afraid. It took months and months to even start to begin to feel and live a new type of normal. With the help of family, friends, and bereavement counseling, I took my crown off the shelf. As I began to shine it, my hope started to return and eventually I began to live a new normal. So, I put my crown back on and began to feel like the queen I was meant to be.

A year after my mom's passing, my sister had to have emergency surgery. She survived, thank God, and came to stay with me while she recovered. For the next nine months, I had to take my crown back off and put it back on the shelf. No longer did I feel like the queen I was supposed to be. Caregiving is an arduous job that leaves little time or thought to selfcare or even wearing a crown. But my God is faithful, and eventually my sister recovered fully and returned to her own home. I looked at my crown on the shelf, and once again picked it up to restore it to its rightful place. Again, my friends, family and church family were there to not only lift me up, but to encourage me and support me through what was another season of doubt, disillusionment, and despair. After all was said and done, my crown was back where it belonged!

I realize that life is full of ups and downs, curve balls, and storms. Sometimes, however; all these things seem to happen at once. For those who don't have a strong support system, may I suggest that you get one and get one quickly. Understand that those closest to you only want the best for you. If you have the gift of discernment, you will know who to call and when to call them. A class I took recently helped me to see that we have different friends for different reasons. Understand, as I do now, that different people play different roles in your life. You may have a friend who will not allow you to wallow in self-pity. That friend will help you out of your slump, sometimes with tough love. It may seem like that person is not being supportive at all because she won't come to your pity party with the "oh everything will be ok" or "just take your time to get over it". She's the friend who's going to put that crown back on your head and have you getting your act together. She loves you with a fierceness of a momma lion protecting her cub and she won't allow you to let whatever is getting you down keep you down.

So, life goes on and my crown slips and slides threatening to come off again. Then here comes the pandemic and throws everything into a tailspin. Off comes the crown and back on the shelf it goes. My one and only niece passed from COVID-19. Didn't see this one coming at all. The shock, pain and disbelief were overwhelming. Not just for me, but for my entire family. See, my sister lost her only child, so I really didn't take the time to dwell on my feelings, I had to be there for her. I felt I had to be strong so I could help her through her time of loss. Once again, I had to rely on other family, friends, and God to help me with this. Not only was my crown on the shelf, but my sister had packed her crown away. I became her protector. I became her ear. I tried to be everything she needed, not realizing that I couldn't be all she needed. As I tried to "fix" her and help her put her crown back on, my crown on the shelf got dustier and dustier.

Through it all, I thank God for the relationship I have with Him and for the support system He has blessed me with. When I go through any type of trauma, loss or hardship, He sends me who I need exactly when I need them. I have one friend in particular who has been there for me through every season I have been through and has traveled every road of good and bad with me. She is indispensable to me – she is the type of friend I pray every sister has! For now, my crown is back where it should be, but there's always tomorrow.

For my sisters who think they have it all together and live in the "I" world; you know, that's the world where you believe only in yourself and what you accomplish all on your own. I hate to be the one to bust your bubble, but the "I" world doesn't exist and for those living in that world, it's not realistic. We all will need help at some point in life. We will all need a shoulder, an ear, a hug. Why not have someone who will help you live in this world where there are loving people who will be glad to assist you to get that crown on. Someone who won't judge you. Someone who will see other options when you think you are all out of options. Someone who will be with you and for you when times are hard.

Miracles still happen every day. Please don't be so full of yourself that you miss the smallest ones. You may have to be the sister to help another sister straighten her crown, or if, God forbid, put her crown back on. I must confess - there have been days in my life that if it wasn't for a sister reaching out to me, I wouldn't even know where my crown was. Pride is a terrible thing. Pride keeps us boxed in the "I" world. Pride will have you thinking that your crown is bigger, brighter and worth more than your sisters. With all that is going on in the world, this is not the time to be prideful. If you need help, don't be ashamed to ask for help. Help is available if you want it. Don't be on the outside looking in. Don't assume that people know you need help. Our crowns are only on correctly when our backs are straight, and our heads are held high.

Finally, be strong enough and humble enough to straighten your sister's crown. I have been in situations where a simple word of encouragement made the difference in a sister's life. I have given a hug to a sister who didn't ask for it but desperately needed a hug. I have listened to a sister vent and not offered a single word. I have stopped in the middle of what I was doing to pray for a sister in need. I have cried for a sister in pain. In short, there are so many ways to straighten a sister's crown without expecting anything in return, except to see her smile. Straightening a sister's crown takes nothing away from you. Do you realize that *that* is your purpose here on earth – to be a blessing. Nothing you can do or say is worth more than being a blessing or encouraging a sister who is down. Sure, you probably have your own cares and concerns and need someone to straighten your crown. You have not because you ask not. Step out on faith. Pray. Read your bible. Do something just for you (it's really ok). Love yourself so you can know how to love someone else. A crown is a thing of beauty, wear it like the adornment it's meant to be. You're not the only one entitled to a crown and neither am I. You can't shine and see me wallowing in the muck and mire. You need me and I need you. Let's make this world a little kinder by helping each other. No, you can't change the world by straightening my crown and I can't either. But, I just might be able to change one sister's world by straightening her crown. She just might pay it forward and do the same – and on and on and on.

My family is continuing to straighten each other's crowns. Yes, we're still going through a healing process, but I am so happy for the opportunity to share with you. I pray you will be inspired to help a sister whose crown is not quite right.

I pray you have a support system of sisters who think it not robbery to straighten the crowns of other sisters. They say it takes a village. Well, let's start a revolution of sisters who are willing and able to straighten the crowns of not just our loved ones, but of any sister in need. Be blessed!

Boundaries
Michele Mekel

It requires neither stone gates thick as they are tall nor coils of electrified concertina wire.

All that's needed is the calcified cage of living bone, surrounding the beating heart—

And, of course, an ample dose of self-respect.

Cherish the Moment!
Tamara N. Harvey

Like many of you, 2020 was a year I will never forget! Last year when we celebrated the New Year and professed our love for one another on Valentine's Day, we would have never guessed that by St. Patricks' Day, we would be on quarantine and curfew. Schools and businesses closed, and those who could, forced to learn and work from home virtually. We had to adjust to a new routine that we thought would be just for a few weeks, but a year later is now the norm. Millions of Americans found themselves unemployed, unequipped to home school their children, and some faced eviction, food insecurity, and the devastating reality of losing loved ones to the Coronavirus.

For me, week by week, I planned our days by helping my children with their school lessons and starting my workday as early as possible. It was hard at first, but I never gave up, and I was proud that my children were able to persevere through this challenging time; and that they were in good spirits as they graduated from elementary school. Even though they could not have their traditional graduation at the school, they could have a virtual one. I will always encourage my children to stand tall and strive to maintain a good spirit every day. But I realize it is hard for all of us. We are now in another school year, and our school district is beginning to return students to the classroom. As a mother, I rely on my faith to make decisions about our well-being. I also depend on the facts (science) from our government to determine if these new guidelines are safe.

My heart goes out to those women who lost their jobs due to COVID-19, especially those who care for our children and serve our communities. As if the staggering number of women unemployed were not enough, some women found themselves victims of sexual violence and domestic abuse. Clearly, women have been adversely affected by the pandemic, but now they are standing up to it. They are slowly returning to the workforce, and with help from the government, maintaining their finances.

I know when my back is up against the wall, I call out for help from God so that I can face my battle with boldness. I dig deep and pull out the strength from within and prepare for my strategy to regroup and bounce back. Personally, the pandemic took an emotional toll on me. At first, I feared the unknown and the possibility of my family and me contracting this deadly virus. I knew that I had to get my mind right and adjust to our new way of living and learning. I also knew that it was up to me to protect my children and ensure we take precautions when we must go out. I knew that I did not have time to be weak; instead, I needed to be strong even when I did not want to be.

To maintain my sanity, I began to meditate daily for about 5-10 minutes in the morning and exercise for at least 30 minutes. Just like many of you, I gained those '15' pandemic pounds, and now I must do something to get them off. I found Pilates, and I love it! I take virtual courses when I can, and I try to book at least one class per week at the local club. Treat yourself! My Mom always told me that after working hard, you must treat yourself. We could not go to the salon during the pandemic, so many of us realized that we could do our hair, manicures, and pedicures. I encourage all of you to invest in yourselves. Read, journal, pray, meditate, walk, drink more water, exercise, draw, paint, sing, start that business. And please remember to rest. Laugh, live, and love!

Last year, I joined *TikTok* like many other forty and over moms and dads, and I am glad I did. The *TikTok* videos are funny, and I have learned so many tips for cleaning, organizing, and decorating my home. Social media has also been an avenue where women have grown their businesses. Millions of those women decided to take the time during the pandemic to take a leap of faith and start their businesses. By showing their work on *TikTok* videos and Instagram photos, billions of dollars of merchandise have sold, and new friends and customers made.

When I saw Cheryl's Instagram post about this anthology, I knew I wanted to be a part of it. So, the first thing I did was write a few haiku poems, then I began to search for bible verses about women, virtue, strength, and a crown. Finally, the week of March 26, 2021, a few days before the deadline, I prayed and decided to write something to go along with the poems. My schedule is so hectic right now with work, school, and chauffeuring my kids around, but I made the time. I cannot stress how important it is for women to be there for each other. For most girls, her mother is her best friend and confidant; I know mine is. There is no love like the love from your mother. Our friends and family also provide us with the relationships we need to survive. I value my friendships and look forward to when we can return to more normalcy to get together and celebrate.

Zoom meetings and celebrations are okay, and so are the drive-by baby showers, but there is nothing like giving and receiving a great big hug.

I hope my words have encouraged you in some way. I want to leave you with this message: We do not know how much time we have on this earth together. Check on your family and friends especially those who live alone. Help your neighbor when you can. Cherish your loved ones, and if possible, mend those broken relationships so your heart can heal and move forward. And if you see a sister who is down for whatever reason, stop and help her straighten her crown.

Peace & Blessings

Try Again
Cheryl Barton

Misery loves company, or so you think;
The ship is going down, do you get off or
just sink.

Life throws you a curveball, you may
want to run;
Why not stick around, your best is yet to
come.

Some paths seem dark and drear, many
have no light;
Don't give up thinking no good is in
sight.

Things may seem bleak every now and
then;
Dust yourself off, rise, stand and try
again.

I've had my own share of being up, then
down;

I know how quickly a smile can turn into
a frown.

I thought about life and how sad it would
be;
If I didn't let go of the heartache, so I set
it free.

Ladies, I know you've heard it before, I'm
preaching to the choir;
But making sure you never give up,
I'll never tire.

I see you hesitate as you whisper, "why
me",
I encourage you to believe in what's
really possible,
I'm asking you to wait and see.

That crown is slighted tilted, but help is
on the way
I'm here to help you straighten it,
I'm here to help you slay.

So when your world seems like it may be

crumbling,
Stick out your hand, place it in mine,
Let me help keep you from stumbling,
I'm here to help you shine.

Nothing beats a fall better than when you
stand and rise,
Your victory will be expected,
It won't be yet another surprise.

I have no doubt that one day, when you
get to that great end,
You will smile and say that it was well
worth it, you know, trying again.

Unlocking Level L
Jill Ocone

Roman Numeral L.

Half of a century.

18,250 days.

438,000 hours.

26,297,460 Minutes.

Somewhere around 1,577,923,200 seconds.

Earlier this year, I celebrated my Semi-Centennial.

To some people, turning 50 is a death sentence.

I blissfully disagree.

Turning 50 is a hell of a lot better than the alternative of staring at the wrong side of the grass.

To commemorate the occasion, I had professional portraits taken with the people I love on the same day I received a special invitation in the mail from AARP welcoming me to "The 50 Club."

I could have taken umbrage and made a scene by ranting and raving and ripping the mailing to shreds, then uncontrollably bawl like a child while stuffing my face with ice cream. Not the wisest choice for someone recently diagnosed with Type-2 Diabetes, another age-related prize alongside the random floater that recently appeared in my left eye.

Instead, I accepted the reality that I am now qualified to be a member of the American Association of Retired Persons, which is one step closer to actual retirement and begin what I have dubbed "Phase 3" of my life.

I happily signed up for membership and now carry my prized AARP membership card in my wallet. I'm a part of the exclusive club that entitles me to a plethora of membership-related discounts. Saving money never goes out of style no matter how many calendars I've lived through, and I even received a wonderful three-piece luggage organizer set as a welcome gift, which I will put to good use after COVID traveling restrictions are lifted.

I have reached the age that renders me eligible for just about every insurance plan advertised on television. You know those commercials that begin with, "If you're between the ages of 50 and 85…"

Yup. I am that target demographic.

I am also the target demographic for the wrinkle reducers, the face lifters, the waist cinchers, the weight loss elixirs, the lip plumpers, and everything else society says I need to waste my money on so I can look twenty or more years younger.

The truth is this: I made it to 50, which is quite an accomplishment, and I look fine just the way I am, thank you very much.

In the words of the immortal Barry Manilow, I made it through the rain.

I survived my self-perpetuated sophomoric recklessness of my twenties when, at times, the bottle was my sole comrade-in-arms. Over time, I realized it was actually a traitorous enemy in disguise, and I left it for dead on the battlefield.

I triumphed over death's many near misses, some the result of poor choices and clouded perceptions, others the result of fate's intervention or maturity.

I rallied and learned to live in balance with the occasional debilitating effects of autoimmune illness and the intermittent yet ravaging side-effects of necessary medication to combat such effects.

I am a champion every morning when I wake up, and I am the victor when I lay my head down each night.

Every one of my wrinkles and scars is both a storyteller and a medal of honor, a collective symbol of my perseverance to this moment, to the here and now.

I may be tired, but I am still here.

I am 50, and I AM STILL HERE.

I am alive. My heart is still beating. My lungs are still working. I am still breathing.

My soul flourishes as my passions, stronger than my pain, fuel my purpose.

My light, it shines while my darkness brightens with insight.

I always do my best, and my best IS enough.

I am resilient, wiser than I was yesterday, and I will be even more enlightened when I awaken tomorrow.

I embrace my idiosyncrasies and regard my flaws as flawsome and my imperfections as perfectly perfect.

I am fabulous, and I am 50.

I am here to unabashedly live out loud, and to love both myself and others unconditionally.

Level L has officially been unlocked, and it's going to be radically phenomenal.

Legacy
Shannon Scott

If today was your last day to live, could you look back and be proud?

Was the time you spent on this earth, used finding your purpose in life?

Did you have the courage to step out on faith and to listen to the little voice that pushes you to move like no one else?

Most of us did not inherit the riches of the land. We fought to make a difference.

To create a lane that we marked out for ourselves, even when the entire world was against us, laughing at us, telling us that what we dream of had already been done.

That we were not the right ones to take that leap because the support level wants to keep us at eye level.

The purpose is found in the pursuit of a dream.

The legacy is made by the lives that it touched.

So, are you going to die with regret or, are you going to manifest a legacy transforming your dreams into reality?

The Miseducation of an Intelligent Black Queen
Treesa "Poesis" Boyce-Gaither

The miseducation of an intelligent black
Queen,
Silenced by everyone when she tried to be
seen.

Born fearless with the strength of the
ancestor's dream,
Standing proud and tall, being great is your
destiny.

Ruling from the throne even on the
battlefield,
I see you "Candace," you even have *Sex
Appeal*!

But don't make them think that's your
worth,
Your skin, hair, lips, and back; you had it
since birth.

They want to be you so bad,
They go to doctors and give them all their cash.

Those culture vultures are manufactured,
Your magic runs naturally through your veins, it can't be recaptured.
Look at everything you accomplished plus so much more,
Listen, don't let them think we're in competition, no one's keeping score.

Standing side by side... front or back, you are protected at every angle,
United by sisterhood, this bond they can't tangle.

Take your place in this world, it's nothing anyone can do... remember Amina, Nanny, Diana Prince, Winnie, Makeda, Angela, Nandi, Cicely, Okoye, Aminatu ...YOU

There's Still Water in the Well
Terry Beamon

Inspired by John 4:1-26

When I think about water, I think about being thirsty, about going out to eat and not wanting anything to drink with my meal but water. I think about the storms we had in the spring and summer and how the water caused the loss of lives and much damage, yet so many people were connecting and praying and providing for others. I think about my niece, "EAT M UP", and how she had advanced in her swimming lessons and how my niece, Cinderella, loves the water spots while on family vacations. Let me not forget how my daughter and I spent so many vacations at beaches in Florida, California, Maryland, Virginia and South Carolina. My daughter also experienced the beaches in Hawaii. I think about how we use so much water washing clothes, bathing, gardening, cleaning our homes, fighting fires, and so much more. But wait, how about the times we spent in the country during the summer with Pop and Grandma and how we would hang out washing soda bottles to get a refund and take the bottles to the store to get some candy. Wow!!! Oh yes, and then there was Uncle Willie's well, that fresh cold water that we would throw the bucket down in that well and hear an echo. But guess what, I baptized the cat and some chickens in the pond near uncle Willie's house. The chickens died and believe me I could have used some of that water to put the fire out when I got a **good beating**...lol

But later, my grandfather introduced me to Jesus. "The Living Water" and my life has never been the same. You see, I myself did not realize, like the woman in the biblical story, would meet a man that knew everything about her without even telling Him a thing. This woman would go to the well early in the morning before most people would get up and she would go and get her water from that well. You see, she was labeled as a "WOMAN OF THE

WORLD" and other women made her feel shameful which is why she went that early to the well. But during one of her visits to the well early one morning, she ran into a man not like any she has ever encountered before. During the conversation, He revealed to her that HE knew her story. He also told her that He was the "Living Water" that could fulfill her every need. You see, we judge people so much without knowing their story. I can relate to this Samaritan Woman, not by being a "WOMAN OF THE WORLD" but by having some voids in my life that I was trying to fulfill with some bad habits of my own.

We ALL have or have had, at some time in our lives, a thirst for something that was not fulfilling our voids. We have all searched hard for that fulfillment and at some time in our lives, we have met a Man named Jesus who filled that void. But just in case you have not, **GO TO YOUR WELL**!!! Because there is **STILL WATER IN THE WELL.** Continue to **THIRST!!!**

One Choice
Michele Mekel

Dead end.
Go back.
Where to?
Impossible!

Think of going back to bed,
then march
magnificently onward,
fierce-looking woman.

Hit the Reset Button
Cheryl Barton

There are days when I find myself going down a rabbit hole and it's a pretty big one. The problem isn't that I'm in that hole, it's that I find it's a quiet, comfortable place. I convince myself that in that hole, I will find peace where nothing about the drama and pressure of the real world can seep in.

When I'm in that hole, I don't have to deal with anyone. I don't have to communicate with the outside world. I can find a little time just for me; something that I find is rare. I'm that person who is often pulled in so many different directions and I try to give a little to everything else, but seldom to me. In some ways, that hole becomes my salvation. In my mind, if I'm in it, no one can find me. I can live in that hole for as long as I want because I find that it gives me some semblance of peace. And then...

In that rabbit hole, there is nothing to do. I don't have a book with me or any music, just dirt all around and when I look up, there is the sky. The view of the sky causes me anxiety. It brings to the surface, my fears and ideal of being unsure of what I am to do in life. The sky represents everything that I felt I was escaping from by getting in that hole. I wasn't in it by accident; it was a purpose-filled jump into the unknown. And then...

When I shut out the world when I'm in the hole, I at first, smile because I think I'm free. I celebrate because in that solitude, nothing and no one is depending on me. The error of my ways doesn't visit me in that hole. I feel like if I can just stay in that hole, I could live like that forever and just be whole. Imagine being in a 'hole' and thinking you can be 'whole'. Have you ever wanted to just be? And then...

When reality sets in, the walls of the hole begin to close in. I start to feel like I'm suffocating just as much, if not more, than I did outside of that hole. The happy feeling of being in that self-imposed small, dense place where life still existed for me, but no real living was taking place, began to feel like a tomb. It felt like a place where things go to die and not live. In that hole, there is no family. There are no friends. There is no creativity and being a writer, constant creativity gives me life. That hole turned my smile into a frown when I realized it's not where I really want to be. And then...

Outside of the hole there is drama and responsibility and I forget that there is also a sense of accomplishment when I look drama and responsibility in the face and give it the finger because through it all, I always seem to persevere. In the hole, there is no room to do anything. I'm in a ball, sitting with my legs and arms crossed, holding myself together because if I let go, I don't know if I can hold myself up. I become frightened of that space, of that hole that I thought, if I could just get to again, I could hit the reset button and start all over again. And then...

The hole begins closing in on me. The dirt that makes up the walls of the hole starts to crumble and it's not a nice place to be. I wonder, what happened to feeling whole in the hole? It's not a comfortable place or a place of peace. It's a temporary escape from a world I will eventually have to get back to or allow the dirty walls to cover and smother me. What happens then is I can't think, I can't breathe; I can't focus. I can't do anything but sit and when I think life is at a standstill because I'm putting everything about it out of my mind in that space, reality is when it rains and the dirt turns to mud and any attempt to get out of the hole becomes futile. I'm now frightened, afraid, scared and I realize real life is not found at the bottom of that hole; it's found by running into life at full speed and focusing on how to find my peace, my solitude without dropping into a place with dirt as walls. And then...

I've been in that hole several times and each time I venture out from it, I'm disappointed that things have not changed; those things that caused me to fall into that realm in the first place still exist and taunt me. They are still there prickling at me, provoking, teasing me, telling me that in the hole or out of it, I'm still the same person struggling to figure out how to smile through the next twenty-four hours. And then...

And then I rise and for the first time in my life. I do so to never throw myself back into that hole again. Instead of sitting any longer, I stand to find that I can touch the surface, just by standing up. I stand, holding my head high, looking up at the sky and around at the world. The sun is shining, I push myself up and out and down on one knee. I count down from five and I take off running. I'm going so fast that people, places and things are blurry images passing by me. At first, I think that there is no destiny on the horizon, but that's not true. I'm running with a quickness to find the reset button. I need a fresh start, one that leads me to face what I couldn't deal with by allowing myself to fall into that hole. And then...Reset!

I know that I'm not the only person who thinks that if I could just find that one place in the world where I can get away from everything and everyone, I would be okay. The trials of life are not meant to cause us pain alone, but to help us realize that all we need is a little reset button in order to energize, rejuvenize and rationalize our way into a better newness. Yes, we all pull away, but never forget to get back to life. Climb out of whatever hole you find yourself in, set new goals and new boundaries for the people in your life and get back to living. And then...Reset!

Find yourself a shovel and don't just put the dirt back in the hole you've just climbed out of. Fill that space with concrete so that digging that hole again and jumping in is never a possibility. Get rid of that option and chose to live again. Don't shut yourself off thinking life is better that way; in that hole. Embrace the reset and when you need to find some time for yourself, find it out in the world in an enjoyable place, not a hole where you can't get out and you won't let anyone in to help you. And then...Reset!

I love a good reset, but I don't want to keep having them again and again. If so, that means I didn't follow my own advice of filling that hole with something more solid than just dirt. Dirt makes it easy for me to claw my way back down to that dark space to escape. I recently allowed myself one last reset and all I see is me winning at this thing called life and so can you. And then...Reset!

And then there is love.
Because you **_Reset!_**

And then there is peace.

Because you *Reset!*

And then there is delight.

Because you *Reset!*

And then there is joy.

Because you *Reset!*

And then there is happiness.

Because you *Reset!*

And then there is harmony.

Because you *Reset!*

And then there is family.

Because you *Reset!*

And then there are friends.

Because you *Reset!*

And then there is the hope of a better today.

Because you *Reset!*

And then there are dreams of tomorrow.

Because you *Reset!*

And then there is creativity.

Because you *Reset!*

And then there is forgiveness of yourself and others.

Because you *Reset!*

And then there is hope.

Because you *Reset!*

And then there is greater.

Because you *Reset!*
And then there is better.

Because you *Reset!*

And then there is restoration.

Because you *Reset!*

And then there is power.

Because you *Reset!*

And then...And then...And then...And then there is *YOU*. A better you. A happier you. A more determined you.

Because you *Reset!*

And then...And then...And then there is a generation who is watching you conquer the things that you fear the most and they find that they too can live without that hole. They will know that there is a reset button for their lives too.

Understand your impact and remember, when you hit that reset button, it's not just for you. It's for those who struggle with everyday life and wonder if anyone has ever made it through.

If this is you, trust that you have before, you will again – just as I have. We will live and thrive together and together, let's hit the reset button.

In the end, there is You!

Let's hit the reset button! If you need me, just call.

Closing
Shannon Scott

A valued woman will create her legacy to gain, her power.

When stepping out on faith, your dreams may be seen only by you.
Everyone is not going to understand your path or the decisions and choices you need to make to get there.
Even failure should be looked at like a lesson and not a curse.
Giving up is not an option because your dream could be someone else's safe space.

Enjoy this excerpt from "A Letter to My Mother", a family-focused inspirational story

"Hey dad, are you here?"

Houston Ray hollered for her father again and again as she entered her parents' home. She had an hour left before her shift began at the hospital where she works as a registered nurse. She hated being late, but when her father called saying he needed to talk to her about an urgent matter, she knew nothing could keep her from coming by to see what was going on.

"He'll be right in Houston," her step-mother Anna said, coming into the room.

"Oh, hi Anna. Do you know what this urgent matter is my dad wants to talk to me about?" she asked.

Houston watched as Anna looked away, not able to look her in the eye. She knew then that Anna knew and she also knew that Anna wouldn't tell her. Whatever it was, it must be serious, she thought.

"Don't quiz your mother when I told you I would tell you when you got here," her father said entering the room.

Nicholas Ray was the greatest man Houston

knew and also the best father any girl could have. She turned at the sound of his voice, smiled and ran into his outstretched arms.

"You were sounding all mysterious on the phone and I was anxious to find out what's so important. You know how you can be all drama-like," she said making fun of the slang her younger twin sisters used.

"I'm going to finish laundry while you two talk," Anna said, in words filled with concern. Houston looked from Anna to her father and noticed he had the same worried look on his face.

"Okay, enough of this, so tell me what's going on," she said, losing patience with not knowing.

As Anna left, Houston joined her father in the sitting room, her favorite place to sit and read as a child growing up.

"Come and sit down Houston," he said, appearing nervous as he clasped his hands together in a manner that let Houston know he had something bad to tell her.

"Just say it since you know I like the bandage on a wound ripped off quickly and not slowly," she said making reference to her desire to always get bad news quick and up front and not have it dragged out.

"Your mother is in a coma in a hospital in California."

Houston was confused considering she'd just seen her mother in the next room. Perhaps her father meant to say another name.

"What are you talking about. Anna seems fine to me."

"Not that mother Houston; I'm talking about your birth mother, Rachel. She's had some kind of accident and is in the hospital and they aren't sure she's going to make it."

Houston stood suddenly, finding it hard to breathe as she tried to wrap her thoughts around his words. She hadn't heard that name in a long time and she'd tried for years to not think about the woman who walked out on her when she was an infant. Her heart began to beat rapidly in her chest at a pace unfamiliar to her. A woman she'd never met, but that she felt close to because her blood ran through her very own veins, was dying before she'd ever been able to set eyes on her.

"Houston, are you okay? Take your time and ask me whatever you need to," she heard her father say calmly.

She paced trying to gather her thoughts, not

knowing where to begin with her questions. There was much she wanted to know.

Through the years her father tried to answer questions about her mother, but she knew he was holding back, not wanting to tarnish the memory of her mother for her. He'd always told her that it wasn't his place to tell her mother's story and that he hoped one day Rachel would tell her own story to Houston, but that day never came and Houston had resolved that she would never get to meet the woman who gave her life.

She turned back to her father, not just to ask questions, but for the comfort she knew she'd find by looking into his face.

"What happened to her?" she asked coming back to sit next to him.

"I don't know all of the details other than she was in a car accident and that her injuries are pretty severe. She slipped into a coma a few days ago, and they aren't offering her family much hope."

Houston's radar went up when she heard her father say the word, 'family'.

"What family? You've always said she didn't have any family?"

Houston remembered her father telling her

when he'd met Rachel many years ago, that she was living with a foster family and that she had no biological family that he knew of.

Her father continued on.

"The family I'm speaking of is her husband, Marcus Ealy and her son Mark."

Houston's reaction to hearing that Rachel had a son showed on her face in a way that put her father's guard up.

"Her name is Rachel Ealy and she's been alive all this time with a husband and a son?" she asked.

"Houston, before you fly off the handle, yes Rachel has a husband and son and until her accident, she was well and living in California. Her son is in his twenties and in the Navy and I knew nothing about him or her husband until yesterday. Let me try to explain as much as I can about what I know based on what I was told."

Houston knew to calm herself down and not get angry or even feel jealous about the fact that a woman who didn't want her desired and had another child, one who got to grow up with her.

"Rachel must have known where we were, but for how long I don't know. Her best friend

Lana came to see me at the office yesterday and at the time, I thought she was a new client when she asked to speak to me. I sat in my office while she explained to me who she was. I should have recognized her since she's an actress. She told me about the accident and that Rachel has been living in California for some years now after spending some time overseas with her husband who recently retired from the military. They made their home in California some years ago. She also mentioned that she was able to locate me because Rachel told her who I was and had also told her about you. She didn't go into detail about how much she knew about you, but she didn't want Rachel to pass away and you not know that she was still alive all this time."

Houston shook her head, not believing that her father was telling her that Rachel was alive all these years, obviously knew where they were and made no effort to contact them.

"I can't believe she's been alive this whole time."

"I know this comes as a shock Houston. Lana told me that the accident happened about a week ago. She's apparently in really bad shape. From what I understand, her husband has agreed to a date of when he will allow them to remove her from life support. Lana told him that she wanted to reach out to you to see if you wanted to fly out to California and then he would make the decision on the date. There is no pressure here for you to do anything and whatever you decide to do, I'm in full support of it. Houston, I know you don't know her and there were a lot of years of hurt that you and I had to work through, so you think on this and if you want to go, I'll go with you, stand with you and comfort you in any way you need. If you decide you don't want to do anything at all, I will respect and support that too."

Nicholas Ray waited, practically holding his breath waiting on his daughter to take it all in. He knew it was painful for her to hear that Rachel had been alive for the past thirty years, all of Houston's life, and had not once tried to reach out and contact them. He didn't care how long it took, he would sit and remain quiet until she let him know how he could help her through this.

"Daddy she could die and it would be life as usual for me since it's like she's been dead for the past thirty years anyway."

She looked to him for support in the way she

was feeling.

"Does that sound too harsh or even morbid? I don't want it to sound that way. I don't know how to react to this. My first thought is to not go and feel the hurt all over again of her being snatched from my life as if she's walking away again. My second thought is, though she is in a coma, I would like to see her before she passes away. I don't know if I would have anything to say, but I'd like the goodbye to be on my terms and not hers like it was thirty years ago. I want to know what you think about what I should do."

Houston grasped her father's hands and as they looked at each other for comfort, she knew that he would give her his honest opinion without judgement.

"It doesn't sound harsh or even morbid for you to feel that way. Your feelings about Rachel are yours. If for no other reason than to look upon her and have the chance to say goodbye, which is something you have been unable to do all these years, I say do it. If this is all you get of Rachel, then this will be all that you will need. God allowed Lana to reach out to me yesterday when I know that she could have let Rachel slip away and die and never tell us about it. This could be exactly what you need to finally get closure, though it's not the closure you'd want. We do have one thing that we have to consider and that is, I don't know the date that her husband will choose to have her removed from life support and your wedding is coming up in a month. I don't want this to put a damper on your special day. I've been looking forward to walking you down the aisle to give you away to Noah. This shouldn't be a cloud over that day."

Houston was set to marry the love of her life, Noah in just over thirty days. She needed to talk to Noah because her mind was made up.

"I know and I need to talk to Noah about all this since it impacts him too. There's a lot to think about and still a lot to do for the wedding."

Her father shook his head in agreement with her.

"Yes, there is. I have a phone number for Lana if you would like to get the latest on Rachel's condition. I told her I would either let her know myself or have you call her with your plans. What are you thinking about doing?" he asked.

Houston thought about what he'd said and

agreed that the little bit of closure she could get from this would-be worth the lifetime of hurt and pain she'd always felt, not knowing why her mother never wanted her.

"I'm going to go see her to say my goodbye. I only have one more week of work before taking the next two months off for the wedding, honeymoon and moving out of my condo and into our new home. I'm going to ask if I can take the extra week and go as soon as possible after I've discussed this with Noah. I'll give Lana a call today to see if the family has made any decisions about life support. I want to get there before they do."

This wasn't the conversation she wanted to eventually have with her father about her birth mother, but she was thankful that he told her. Lana didn't have to come all this way to tell him about Rachel and he didn't have to tell her. He could have let her live her life never knowing, especially if Rachel passed away. As far as she was concerned, in her mind, Rachel had died years ago. That thought gave her comfort instead of the other option which was that Rachel was happily living a life and never thought about the daughter she left behind.

"Thank you, Daddy, for loving me so much.

I know hearing that Rachel has been alive all these years is as much a shock for you as it is for me. She left us thirty years ago and never looked back. I don't know why, but I'm hoping to get some peace and understanding from my visit to see her. I know you want to be there with me and for me through all of this, but I want to go alone. I have so much I want to think about and I'd like to take some time for reflection. I may stay more than one day and Anna and my sisters need you here. I promise I will call you often and anytime you want to check on me, I will have my phone on day and night. Let me talk to Lana and Noah and then I'll let you know my plans. I hope you're okay with that."

Houston wanted to tread lightly and didn't want her father's feelings hurt knowing that even after all these years and the good life and unconditional love that he and Anna have given her, that she still longed to see Rachel.

"I'm following your lead on this and I will be here in any capacity that you need. Promise me that before you board a plane going anywhere, that you will take some time and pray about forgiveness. I've told you many times in the past that even though I was hurt when she left us, I forgave her a long time ago because you can't live a life consumed with hate for someone because they didn't choose the life you wanted them to choose. Whatever Rachel's reasons were, they were her reasons and though I know you missed having a mother in your life before I married Anna, God has blessed your life tremendously. Pray for clarity and understanding and don't question why God has made the decision to call Rachel home before you can have a chance to have her as a part of your life. Know that He is responsible for granting you this little time with Rachel, so make it count. I love you and day or night, you pick up that phone if you need to hear my voice and if you need me there, I'll be on the first flight out."

Houston nodded her head as a few tears fell to her cheek. She loved her father and was thankful that he had always been there for her, never giving up on her.

"Thank you, Daddy, and because I've watched you live your life without regret, without hatred or anger over Rachel, I promise you I will pray about forgiveness and understanding. Thank you for showing me early in my life who God is and because of that,

I know I can make it through this and will be able to walk away without any hatred in my heart. I believe I need to do this in order to finally put closure to the unknown even if it's just to see her and not hear from her."

She stood to leave and as her father stood, she hugged him with a tight bear hug. He has always put her first, took care of her and never gave her reason to doubt that he loved her more than anything. They've always had a special bond and because of that, she knew he would help see her through this.

"I love you Dad."

"I love you too, Houston. You have always been that breath of fresh air that makes everything in my life worth living. I'm proud of you and we will both make it through this. I'll tell your sisters you were here since they're still in school."

"Tell them I'll call them later. I want to know what they think of their dresses for the wedding. They had final fittings yesterday and they looked gorgeous. I'll go give Anna a hug before I leave. I know I don't have to tell her, but I want her to know how much I love her, especially with all of this with Rachel. Nothing and no one could ever take her place in my life as the mother who gives me love and support. She stepped into her role as my mother and I'm thankful for her."

Get "A Letter to my Mother" in paperback and download
https://www.crbarton.com/a-letter-to-my-mother

Contributing Writers Biographies

∽∾∿◈∿∾∽

Cheryl Barton

Cheryl Barton lives in Maryland and in her spare time she loves to read espionage, crime and romance novels, cook, watch Science Fiction movies, spend time with family and friends and enjoy Maryland steamed crabs. Cheryl is celebrating 30 years as a federal government employee and loves writing romance novels when she's not working.

Cheryl is the author of over 40 romance novels, 5 inspirational novels and is proud of 4 book compilation projects with several other incredible women called, *"One Sister Away: Encouraging Words from One Sister to Another"* – a series of books meant to encourage, empower and inspire other women.

People often ask Cheryl which book is her favorite of all of those she's written. While she finds it hard to select one favorite, she still looks to her first novel, *Bachelor Not for Sale*, if she had to pick a favorite because it was her first novel and the one that inspired her to continue writing.

In addition to writing, Cheryl started her own woman-owned, independent book publishing company, *Cheryl Barton Publishing* and has published books by several other authors. More information can be found on her company's website at www.crbarton.com.

Cheryl was a 2019 Finalist for the Emma Award writing contest given by the Romance Slam Jam and a 2018 Finalist for the Literary Trailblazer of the Year award by the Indie Author Legacy Award. Cheryl is a member of the Romance Writers of America – National Chapter, the Maryland Romance Writers and the Contemporary Romance Writers groups.
Indulge in more romance and inspirational novels by visiting her website at www.cherylbarton.net and connect with Cheryl on Facebook, Twitter and Instagram.

Nichole M. Wallace

Nichole M. Wallace is a native of Baltimore, Maryland and a licensed minister of the Gospel at Morning Star Baptist Church of Woodlawn, Maryland, under the leadership of Bishop Dwayne C. Debnam. She is on staff at the church's Renaissance Christian Counseling Center as a Clinical Therapist. As a licensed minister and advocate at heart, she specializes in restoration, recovery, and reconciliation for those impacted by trauma associated with child maltreatment, domestic violence, and divorce and separation. She is also well trained in the areas of human trafficking and LGBQT.

Nichole is a graduate of Coppin State University and the University of Maryland School of Social Work where she specialized in working with Families and Children. Having over 25 years of social work experience, she is currently a Supervisory Program Specialist for the Department of Health and Human Service's Office of Refugee Resettlement. Nichole is excited about how her vocation leads to her work in ministry and the community.

In 2021, she launched Rooted In Promise L.L.C. Rooted In Promise offers trauma-based training and consultation services for those seeking restoration from life's adversities. Nichole considers all that she does as an opportunity to be the hands and feet that God uses to equip others for change. Every time she hears Luke 4:18 "The Spirit of the Lord is on me, because he has anointed me to proclaim good news to the poor. He has sent me to proclaim freedom for the prisoners and recovery of sight for the blind, to set the oppressed free", her spirit quickens.

Nichole is the proud wife of Alan E. Wallace, mother of Steven, Alexaundria and Amanda Leonard, and bonus mom to Alan, Taylor, Makaila, and Noah Wallace.

Sally Quon

Sally Quon is a writer and photographer, rediscovering her voice after a long confinement. She has been published in numerous anthologies, including "Voicing Suicide," Ekstasis Editions, and "I Don't Cry Anymore," Liminal Press.

Sally is an associate member of the League of Canadian Poets. Her personal blog, https://featherstone-creative.com is where she posts her back-country adventures, photos and stories.

JoAnn Wilson

JoAnn Wilson was born and raised in Baltimore, Maryland. She received her education in the Baltimore City public school system. She started and ended her career with the Federal Government where after 37 years of public service, she retired in 2009 to join the community of retired persons.

Writing has always given her a sense of peace and balance. She can give voice to her thoughts and ideas through the words she puts on paper.

Two of her crowning achievements were having two books, "Pondering" and "Still Pondering" published. JoAnn has been the contributing writer in several other book anthologies. To get a copy of JoAnn published books, contact her at joawilson51@hotmail.com

Terry Beamon

Terry Beamon is a wife and mother and blessed to have this assignment in her life. She is grateful that God chose her for this assignment. If anyone had asked Terry, 49 years ago, what she wanted to be, she would have said a lawyer. She wanted to change the way minorities were treated and to also show them that they are just as important as anyone else. That was not the path that God had for Terry, but one thing she knows for sure and that is that she loves encouraging those others have given up on and those who have given up on themselves. She has always had a passion to journal and write and hopes that her writings will bless and encourage others. Terry is thankful for the doors that God has opened and closed in her life. He continues to blow her mind.

Tamara Harvey

Tamara Harvey is a career Federal Government employee and author. In her debut book, *"I Love Hate My Hair"* (My Journey with Alopecia), she shares what it has been like to lose her hair as a young woman and how she has managed to pay for and cover it over the past two decades. She followed up with another non-fiction book, *"I'll Have a Martini Please!"* wherein she describes a day-in-the-life of a busy wife and mom, using hashtags and daily accounts with her family and friends. This book also provides a sample of her free form and haiku poetry. In 2020, Tamara published her first poetry book, *"MyKu"* (A collection of Haiku Poetry), which includes 200 poems on various topics.

Tamara is enrolled in an online Bachelor's to Master's program to obtain her degrees in Professional Studies and Healthcare Management. She is a member of the Black Writers' Guild of Maryland and she lives in Baltimore County, Maryland.

Michele Mekel

Living in Happy Valley, Michele Mekel wears many hats of her choosing: writer and editor; educator and bioethicist; poetess and creatrix; cat herder and chief can opener; witch and woman; and, above all, human. Her work has appeared in various academic and creative publications, including having her poetry featured on Garrison Keillor's *The Writer's Almanac*. She is also a co-principal investigator for the *Viral Imaginations: COVID-19* project (viralimaginations.psu.edu). Michele can be found on Instagram @ShaktiEnergy.

Jill Ocone

Jill Ocone is a senior writer for *Jersey Shore Magazine* and content editor for several Jersey Shore Publications annual guidebooks. Her work has been published in *Harness* Magazine, Exeter Publishing's *From the Soil* hometown anthology, Red Penguin Books' *'Tis the Season: Poems for Your Holiday Spirit*, *American Writers Review-A Literary Journal* (2020 and 2019 volumes), *Art in the Time of Covid-19*, *Everywhere* magazine, *School Leader*, *American Cheerleader*, NJEA.org, and *The Sun*, among others. In addition to a writer, she is also a high school journalism educator. When Jill isn't writing or teaching, you might find her searching for sea glass along the beach, fishing with her husband, making memories with her nieces and nephews, or laughing with her family and friends. Visit Jill online at jillocone.com, on Instagram and Facebook at @jillocone, and on Twitter at @jill_ocone.

Shannon Scott

Shannon Scott was born on March 5, 1991 in Baltimore, Maryland. She created Climbing and Maintaining in 2021 to help women find power in words and embrace who they are. She is the author of *The Rainbows of My Clouds* and enjoys writing poetry and urban novels. Check out Shannon's book on Amazon.

Treesa "Poesis" Boyce-Gaither

Treesa is a Caribbean-American creative writer who resides in Baltimore County, Maryland. Her hobbies include spending time with family, doing arts and crafts, watching action/suspense/science-fiction movies, reading a variety of books ranging from comic books, self-help, and science-fiction to biographies. Treesa was a contributing writer in the popular, *"One Sister Away; Encouraging Word from One Sister to Another"* book compilation project.

Treesa has a Bachelor's Degree in English Literature and enjoys writing poetry but has aspirations of becoming science fiction novelist. Treesa is married with three kids.

~~Check out these inspirational novels now available for your reading pleasure~~

Girl Dad
By Cheryl Barton
www.amazon.com/author/cherylbarton

Cyrus Jackson went from being a man who survived the streets of Washington, D.C., a local gangster, hoodlum and at one time, drug king-pin, known to put gut-wrenching fear into the hearts and minds of everyone he encountered, to a father who fought the system to get custody of his daughter, Shiloh.

Cyrus hadn't known of Shiloh's existence, but the moment he set eyes on her, knowing she had no one in the world to love her, he couldn't walk away even when the system found him unworthy. He set out on a journey to prove them wrong and to bring light to the eyes of his beautiful little girl. He never wanted her to be or feel alone again.

Rescue Me
By Cheryl Barton
www.amazon.com/author/cherylbarton

Marissa Ballard is "Delilah", an exotic dancer who is living a life of shame in the eyes of her family and finally, herself. She doesn't like who she has become or how far down her life has spiraled for a man she thought loved her when he only saw her dollar value. She wants out and desires to take her life back and to mend her broken relationship with her parents, yet their cold reception is a reminder of their disappointment in her life's choices including turning her back on her daughter, Lacey.

Police Officer, Roman Hale's heart never healed five years after losing his young wife to cancer. His profession no longer gives him hope that he's making a difference in the lives of those he encounters on the streets of Philadelphia. His routine seems aimless and he longs for a new lease on life.

Marissa and Roman's lives intersect and together they form a friendship built on courage, hope and faith for a new beginning not just individually, but together as one when God arrives just in time, not to rescue them, but to send them to rescue each other.

Release Me
By Cheryl Barton
www.amazon.com/author/cherylbarton

Raynard: I heard you can sing.
Zoe: Like you've never heard before.
Raynard: Show me and I'll make you a star.
Zoe: Sit back, listen and then get your check book ready.

Zoe Hamilton had no idea that those words to music executive, Raynard Black, would come back to haunt her in her quest to use her melodious voice for more than singing in church. She wanted to be a star and was willing to sacrifice her dignity and the love and advice of her family in order to achieve it.

Other inspirational novels from Cheryl Barton Publishing

One Sister Away: Encouraging Words from One Sister to Another, Volumes 1, 2, 3 & 4
https://www.crbarton.com/one-sister-away-series

Check out other authors at Cheryl Barton Publishing
https://www.crbarton.com/authors

https://www.crbarton.com/kyle-s-berkley
https://www.crbarton.com/bonita-porter
https://www.crbarton.com/f-lafon-porter
https://www.crbarton.com/shanise-shaw
https://www.crbarton.com/dr-lisa-m-weah
https://www.crbarton.com/joann-wilson

About the Publisher

Cheryl Barton Publishing, LLC

Cheryl Barton Publishing, LLC is a dynamic woman-owned, small independent book publishing company. We proudly hail from Maryland and our foundation is based on the belief that there is a writer in all of us, so just do it! Let us help you get moving toward that writing dream today!

Our company motto is, *"Your Dreams Are Safe in Our Hands"* and we stand behind that.

For more information on the services provided by Cheryl Barton Publishing, LLC and to see other book selections, visit our website at www.crbarton.com.